PRECIOUS STONES

FROM THIS EARTH

William Russell

The Rourke Corporation, Inc
Vero Beach, Florida 32964

PHOTO CREDITS
© William Russell: title page, p. 12, 13, 17, 18;
courtesy Diamond Promotion Service: cover, p. 4, 7, 8, 10, 15, 21

Library of Congress Cataloging-in-Publication Data

Russell, William, 1942–
   Precious Stones / by William Russell.
      p. cm. — (From this earth)
   Includes index
   ISBN 0-86593-361-8
      1. Precious Stones—Juvenile literature. [1. Precious Stones.]
I. Title II. Series.
QE392.2.R87 1994
553.8—dc20
                                                          94-506
                                                          CIP
Printed in the USA   AC

TABLE OF CONTENTS

PRECIOUS STONES

Precious stones are hard, colorful, rocklike objects of great value and beauty. They are often used as jewelry.

The best-known precious stones are diamonds. Emeralds, opals, sapphires, rubies, turquoise and topaz are also among the well-known precious stones.

Many objects that look like precious stones are made of plastic or glass. True precious stones, sometimes called gemstones, are found in nature. Most precious stones are **minerals** of one kind or another.

Diamonds are not only rare, they are the hardest material in nature

MINERALS

Minerals are certain solid materials that exist naturally in the Earth. Many minerals are made up of combinations of materials. The mineral salt, for example, is made of sodium and chloride.

Minerals take many different forms. Salt feels sandlike. Precious stones, however, are hard and solid. They can be polished to be smooth, bright and beautiful.

Diamonds and other precious stones are cut and polished to be bright and beautiful

FINDING PRECIOUS STONES

Precious stones are usually found in or with rock. Certain kinds of precious stones are found in certain kinds of rocks. Don't expect to find diamonds in your backyard!

Like the rocks around them, precious stones form over millions of years. Natural forces underground, such as heat, pressure and mineral-rich water, help make precious stones.

Dynamite blasts rock into small pieces at a diamond mine in Botswana, a country in southern Africa

DIAMONDS

Diamonds in bright light glitter with rainbow color. A diamond may look like crystal glass, but it is much harder. Diamonds, in fact, are the hardest material in nature.

Beautiful and rare, diamonds are popular jewels in rings, bracelets, earrings and necklaces. They are also used in quite another way—for grinding and cutting other hard materials.

Diamonds sparkle with rainbow color

An ivory elephant wears a blanket of gold, sapphires, emeralds and other gems at the Lizzadro Museum of Lapidary Art in Elmhurst, Illinois

Sapphires glitter in a snakelike bracelet of gold

DIAMONDS IN THE GROUND

Diamonds form deep in the ground. Extreme heat and pressure there amazingly change small amounts of a common material called carbon into diamonds. (A more familiar form of carbon is the black matter that remains after a fire.)

Most diamonds are taken from Australia and a few of the African nations. Thousands of pounds of rock have to be smashed before **miners** find just a diamond or two.

Diamonds are mined on five continents, usually from deep in the ground or from under the sea

OPALS AND EMERALDS

Opals are precious stones that nature makes from the same "recipe" as sand. Like diamonds, opals show dazzling colors in bright light. Opals, however, are not nearly as hard as diamonds.

Emeralds are brilliant green stones. They are a form of the mineral beryl. A perfect emerald can be more valuable than a diamond of the same size.

Columbia, India and South Africa are major emerald producers. The best opals come from Australia.

Like other precious stones, opals are usually found in certain kinds of rock

RUBIES AND SAPPHIRES

Under different conditions, the same material can take on very different forms. Remember carbon? It can become a diamond, a lump of coal or many other things.

Rubies and sapphires are both forms of the mineral corundum. Rubies, however, are generally red. Sapphires are usually blue.

Next to diamonds, rubies and sapphires are nature's hardest material.

Many rubies and sapphires are taken from rocks in Burma.

The blue sapphire and red ruby are different forms of the same mineral

CUTTING PRECIOUS STONES

Precious stones in nature are rough and unpolished. Crafts people called **lapidaries** work on them before they are sold as jewelry or decorations.

Lapidaries cut precious stones with special tools and polish them. A lapidary can cut a gem into any number of shapes. The kind of stone and its size help decide how it will be cut.

A diamond "marker" decides how the stone should be cut and marks it with Indian ink

THE VALUE OF PRECIOUS STONES

Precious stones, even of the same mineral, are never identical. Nature has given each stone a special identity.

How do the people who work with polished gemstones decide a stone's value? They consider several things, including a stone's weight, color and form. How "perfect" a stone is also weighs heavily on its value. One diamond may be much more valuable than another diamond of equal weight, for example.

Glossary

lapidary (LAP uh dar ee) — a cutter or polisher of precious stones; the art of cutting precious stones

miner (MY ner) — one who works in a mine

mineral (MIN er uhl) — any of several natural, non-living materials which occur in the Earth

INDEX